RULING THE COURT

Basketball's Biggest Wins

JAIME WINTERS

CRABTREE
Publishing Company
www.crabtreebooks.com

Author
Jaime Winters

Editors
Marcia Abramson, Kelly Spence

Proofreader
Wendy Scavuzzo

Photo research
Melissa McClellan

Design
T.J. Choleva

Cover Design
Samara Parent

Prepress Technician
Tammy McGarr

Production coordinator
Margaret Amy Salter

Written and produced for
Crabtree Publishing by BlueApple*Works* Inc.

Consultant
Greg Verner, President, Ontario Basketball

Cover image:
2015 NBA Champions, Golden State Warriors

Photographs
Cover: AP Images: Paul Sancya
Interior: Carlyn Iverson: p 4, 5 bottom; Bigstock: © Photo Works (p 16);
iStock: © GoodLifeStudio (p 30); Keystone Press: © Nuccio Dinuzzo (p 8 top);
© Imago (p 9 top); © Al Diaz (p 10); © Phil Masturzo (title page middle left,
p 11 right); © Anthony Nesmith (p 13 top); © Kendall Shaw (p 15); © Lexington Herald-
Leader (p 18); © Del Mecum (title page middle right, p 19 left);
© Gokturk Yagiz (p 21); © Harry E. Walker (p 25 top); © DS7 (p 25 bottom);
© Photofest: p 22 left, 22 middle; Shutterstock.com: © Eric Broder Van Dyke
(title page) © Africa Studio (basketball behind page numbers; © Torsak Thammachote (TOC);
© Danny Smythe TOC bottom; © Dewitt (texture background); © Brocreative (page top
left); © Eugene Sergeev (page top border); © prophoto14 (page bottom border); © Slavoljub
Pantelic (Slam Dunk photo); © Aspen Photo (p 18–19 top, 18–19 bottom); © Photo Works
(p 19 top); © Marcos Mesa Sam Wordley (p 20 left, 20 right); © Aitor Bouzo Ateca (p 28);
Zumapress.com: © Steve Lipofsky (p 8 bottom); Public Domain: p 5 top, p 6 left, p 7 left,
p 7 top, p 9 bottom, p 11 left, p 14 left, p 14 right, p 17 top, p 22 middle; Library of Congress:
Hersey Photo Service (p 6–7 top); p 6 bottom; Johnston (Frances Benjamin) Collection (p 6);
National Library of France: (p 6–7 bottom); Creative Commons: Michael Barera (p 10–11 top);
Dave Winer (p 10–11 bottom); Matteo Della Malva (p 11 top right); Joe Bielawa (p 12); Danny
Karwoski (p 13 bottom); Sphilbrick (p 17 bottom); Sphilbrick (p 19 right); David Holt (p 22–23
top); &DC (p 22–23 bottom); Keith Allison (p 22 right, 29 bottom); Tim Shelby (p 23 top, 23
bottom); Christopher Johnson (p 24); Hawkeye7 (p 26 left, 26 right); cdephotos
(p 27 top); Jazi131 (p 27 bottom); edclintongo20 (p 29 top)

Library and Archives Canada Cataloguing in Publication

Winters, Jaime, author
    Ruling the court : basketball's biggest wins / Jaime Winters.

(Basketball source)
Includes index.
Issued in print and electronic formats.
ISBN 978-0-7787-1559-7 (paperback).--
ISBN 978-0-7787-1537-5 (bound).--ISBN 978-1-4271-7755-1 (pdf).--
ISBN 978-1-4271-7751-3 (html)

    1. Basketball--Tournaments--United States--Juvenile literature.
2. Basketball--Tournaments--Juvenile literature. I. Title.

GV885.59.N37W56 2015   j796.323'640973   C2015-903200-8
                                      C2015-903201-6

Library of Congress Cataloging-in-Publication Data

Winters, Jaime.
    Ruling the court : basketball's biggest wins / Jaime Winters.
      pages cm. -- (Basketball source)
    Includes index.
    ISBN 978-0-7787-1537-5 (reinforced library binding : alk. paper) --
ISBN 978-0-7787-1559-7 (pbk. : alk. paper) --
ISBN 978-1-4271-7755-1 (electronic pdf) --
ISBN 978-1-4271-7751-3 (electronic html)
    1. Basketball--History--Juvenile literature. 2. Basketball--
Tournaments--History--Juvenile literature. I. Title.

GV885.1.W557 2016
796.323--dc23
                                    2015021983

Crabtree Publishing Company

Printed in Canada/082015/BF20150630

www.crabtreebooks.com   1-800-387-7650

Published in Canada
Crabtree Publishing
616 Welland Ave.
St. Catharines, ON
L2M 5V6

Published in the United States
Crabtree Publishing
PMB 59051
350 Fifth Avenue, 59th Floor
New York, New York 10118

Published in the United Kingdom
Crabtree Publishing
Maritime House
Basin Road North, Hove
BN41 1WR

Published in Australia
Crabtree Publishing
3 Charles Street
Coburg North
VIC 3058

CONTENTS

TAKE IT TO THE NET!

BASKETBALL IS BORN

What makes basketball unlike any other major league sport? It didn't originate from an ancient sport or game. Basketball was invented in 1891 to give an **unruly** gym class in Springfield, Massachusetts, a fun new sport to play during the cold winter months.

HOOPS' INVENTOR

When a bratty gym class at the **YMCA** (the Y) in Springfield made two teachers quit, a young teacher named James Naismith was up for the challenge. The young teacher thought the problem was the boring exercises the students were doing—not the students themselves. Naismith, a soccer, rugby, and track star from McGill University in Montreal, Canada, decided to shake things up with indoor football. But it was too rough. When indoor soccer and lacrosse failed, too, Naismith decided he needed a new game to try.

Using a soccer ball and peach baskets, James Naismith invented basketball in 1891. His boss at the YMCA gave him two weeks to create a game that did not require a lot of space or expensive equipment.

THE KIDS GET GAME

Naismith remembered playing a childhood game called Duck on a Rock. To play, one player guards a rock, called the "duck," which is placed on top of a larger stone. The other players try to knock the duck off the rock by tossing rocks at it. Inspired, Naismith wrote out 13 rules for a new game. The next day, he posted them on the bulletin board and nailed two peach baskets 10 feet (3 meters) above the gym floor. He told the class the object of the game was to shoot a ball into their opponent's basket. He tossed a soccer ball into the air, two teams jumped up for it, and the game began. Only one player scored a basket, but the class was hooked!

Naismith (top right) went on to start the basketball program at the University of Kansas. This picture was taken with his 1898 team. After nine years as a coach, he became the university's athletic director.

SLAM DUNK!

Baskets got backboards in the 1890s to keep fans from blocking shots. Once backboards became part of the game, players started making **bank shots** off them.

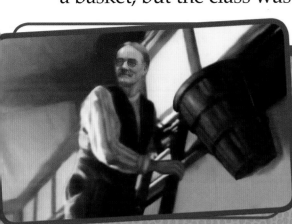

Early games had to pause while referees fetched the ball out of the peach basket.

HOOPS AND LADDERS

Early b-ball was played with a soccer ball. When the ball landed in the basket, a referee had to climb a ladder to remove it. A metal hoop and net soon replaced the basket. In 1906, a hole was cut in the net so the ball would drop through.

RISE OF BASKETBALL

Hoops soon spread from the Y to colleges across North America. But the game needed **standard** rules and a **stable** pro league to take it to the next level.

RULES OF THE GAME

As hoops popped up everywhere, so did questions about the rules and situations for which there were no rules. In 1905, 15 colleges formed the first basketball rules committee to develop rules. In 1910, the National Collegiate Athletic Association (NCAA) started governing college sports, and hoopsters everywhere began playing by their rules.

The North Carolina Tar Heels, one of the first college hoops teams, have won more than 2,000 games since 1910.

Women started playing basketball at Smith College in Massachusetts in 1983.

RISE OF THE NBA

In 1896, more than 600 fans bought tickets to the first pro game. After that, many pro leagues formed but most soon **folded**. The pro game didn't take off until 1946, when a bunch of hockey arena owners thought basketball could take their profits "above the rim." The owners formed the Basketball Association of America (BAA). In 1949, the BAA became the National Basketball Association (NBA) and took the game to the next level.

George Mikan came out of DePaul University in 1946 to become one of basketball's first superstars. His nickname was "Mr. Basketball."

THE WORLD GETS GAME

In 1932, the first international basketball meeting took place. People from 10 countries standardized the rules and formed the International Basketball Federation (FIBA). More people around the world were shooting hoops. Four years later, basketball made its first Olympic appearance. Twenty three nations entered the competition, making b-ball the largest team sport of the 1936 Olympic Games.

SLAM DUNK!

The U.S. won the first Olympic gold medal for basketball, Canada won the silver, and Mexico took the bronze.

JOE **FORTENBERRY**

Joe Fortenberry, a captain on the 1936 U.S. Olympic team, may have been the first player to dunk a basketball. At nearly 6 ft 8 in (2 m), he was very tall for a man in the 1930s.

MIGHTY NBA

Once the NBA got rolling, pro basketball began to take off. As the level of play rose up, so did the number of teams and the **caliber** of competition. Check out how the NBA works today.

HOOP DIVISIONS

Today, the NBA has 30 teams in cities across North America. Each team belongs to the Eastern Conference or the Western Conference, depending on its location or region. Each conference has 15 teams, which are divided into three groups of five teams each. These groups are called divisions. The Eastern Conference holds the Atlantic, Central, and Southeast divisions. While the Western Conference, holds the Pacific, Northwest, and Southwest divisions.

The Chicago Bulls became legendary in the 1990s when superstar Michael Jordan (bottom) and fellow hall of famer Scottie Pippen (left) led them to six NBA titles. The Bulls helped increase the popularity of the NBA.

TOP B-BALL GAME

During the regular season, each NBA team plays 82 games—41 at home and 41 on the road. Fans all over the world watch them on TV and online. In 2013, a record-setting 92 NBA players came from 39 different countries. Teams **vie** for playoff spots in the end-of-season NBA championships. NBA squads also compete against squads from other countries in the NBA Global Games. Each year, NBA teams travel outside the U.S. and Canada to play each other or a club from another country. The Global Games help the NBA gain fans all over the world.

German professional basketball club Alba Berlin upset the San Antonio Spurs in a 2014 Global Game.

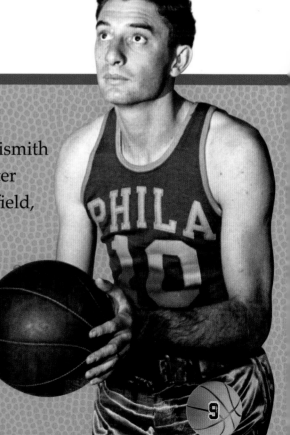

BASKETBALL HALL OF FAME

Hoops history bounces off the walls at the Naismith Memorial Basketball Hall of Fame. Named after b-ball's inventor, the Hall is located in Springfield, Massachusetts, where the game was born. It holds artifacts, such as early balls, baskets, and rule books, and honors history's greatest players.

*Joe Fulks was one of the first players to make **jump shots**, and one of the first named to the Hall of Fame. "Jumping Joe" played for the Philadelphia Warriors from 1946 to 1954.*

9

NBA FINALS

Winning the NBA Finals is the ultimate dream of every NBA team. But getting to the Finals isn't easy. It takes guts, grit, and teamwork to go the distance.

WINNER TAKES IT ALL

All season long, the NBA's 30 teams hit the court to shoot hoops against one another. They work hard to win as many games as possible to earn a spot in the end-of-season playoffs. But only 16 teams secure spots—eight from each conference. These squads then play a best-of-seven games series against those in their conference. The first team to win four of the seven games advances to the next round. The conference winners then face off in the NBA Finals for the championship trophy. Finals champs also receive a championship ring studded with diamonds.

The San Antonio Spurs in the West and the Miami Heat in the East advanced to the 2014 Finals. The Spurs beat Miami, four games to one, to earn their fifth NBA championship.

TROPHY OF CHAMPIONS

It's shiny and bold and covered in gold! The Larry O'Brien NBA Championship Trophy looks like a golden basketball about to drop through a hoop. Made of gold-covered sterling silver, it's no trinket. The trophy stands 2 feet (61 cm) tall and weighs 14.5 pounds (6.6 kg). A new one is made for the NBA Finals every year. That way, the winning team gets to keep it and show it off.

In 1977, the Portland Trail Blazers became the first NBA champions to take home a Finals Trophy they could keep. Star Bill Walton (left) and coach Jack Ramsay carried it together.

In the 2015 NBA Finals, the Western Conference champion Golden State Warriors defeated the Eastern Conference champion Cleveland Cavaliers for the Warriors' fourth NBA championship in the franchise's history.

NAME THAT TROPHY

The golden NBA trophy has gone by three different names. It started out as the NBA Finals Trophy, which was changed to the Walter A. Brown Trophy in 1964 to honor the first owner of the Boston Celtics. In 1984, it was renamed for Larry O'Brien, the **NBA commissioner** who retired that year.

WNBA CHAMPIONS

Women have hoops dreams of their own. Every year, pro players dream of winning the Women's National Basketball Association (WNBA) Finals.

WOMEN GET A LEAGUE

In 1996, the U.S. women's national team toured the world, slaying all the competition on the court. When they came home to the U.S., they won the gold metal at the Atlanta Olympics. Fans went crazy, **clamoring** for more. The WNBA was born. Today, the league has 12 teams. Each one belongs to the Eastern or Western Conference, depending on its location. During the regular season, each team plays 34 games—17 at home and 17 on the road. They all have the same goal—to win as many games as possible to make it to the end-of-season playoffs.

Superstar Maya Moore won two NCAA championships at Connecticut, then joined the Minnesota Lynx in 2011 and earned Rookie of the Year. She has won two WNBA titles, 2013 Finals MVP, 2014 League MVP, and an Olympic gold.

WNBA FINALS

WNBA competition is fierce. Only eight teams reach the playoffs. The squads then go head-to-head with the other teams in their conference in a best-of-three games series. The winner of each series advances to the next round. The conference winners square off in the WNBA Finals, and the first team who wins three out of five games is crowned the champions. The winning team receives the basketball-shaped Championship Trophy, and each player receives a championship ring glistening with diamonds.

The Phoenix Mercury, one of the WNBA's original teams, set a record for wins in a season with 29 in 2014. They followed up by winning their third WNBA championship.

ALL-STAR GAME

Every year, star players come out for the WNBA and NBA All-Star Games. Each game pits the top stars of the Eastern Conference against the top stars of the Western Conference. Fans play a starring role, too, by voting to choose the stars for each team's starting lineup.

Tina Thompson had made 9 WNBA All-Star Game appearances and led the WNBA in all-time scoring with 7,488 points when she retired in 2013.

MEN'S COLLEGE CHAMPS

Once college kids picked up basketball, they rocked the court. Check out how the men's national college basketball championships became one of the hottest sports around.

EAST VS. WEST

In 1939, college basketball coaches in the Midwest were angry. The East Coast, in particular New York, was hogging all the action. The city had invited the top college teams in the country to a b-ball contest—the National Invitation Tournament (NIT)—that spring. Determined to create some action of their own, the coaches ran a competing tournament that set the top college team from the East against the top college team from the West.

Bill Walton, who went on to star for Portland in the NBA, dazzled in the 1973 NCAA championship game by making 21 of 22 field goals and scoring 44 points for UCLA.

UCLA won its seventh NCAA championship in a row in 1973, which no other team has done before or since. Legendary head coach John R. Wooden led the team to 10 titles in 12 years.

1973 NCAA Champions

FROM FLOP TO TOP

The coaches' tournament was a flop. But the NCAA agreed to run it the following year. The NCAA advertised the tournament as the official championship of college basketball. The **ploy** worked. The NCAA championship tournament soon gained the same respect as the NIT. It became a huge hit with fans, and even started to draw more fans than the NIT. Today, the NCAA tournament is held every year in March, and it's one of the biggest, most famous, and most popular sports events around. Fans tune in to the TV broadcast from all over the world.

SLAM DUNK!

Eight teams competed in the tournament that gave birth to the national college championships. Today, 68 teams compete and fans try to predict the outcome of every game.

Center Frank Kaminsky helped take the Wisconsin Badgers to the 2015 NCAA championship game. He was named the 2015 Naismith College Player of the Year.

THE NAISMITH COLLEGE PLAYER OF THE YEAR

The Atlanta Tipoff Club, a group of super-fans, started honoring the Naismith College Player of Year for men's basketball in 1969. A women's award was added in 1983. Coaches, school officials, and media members help the club select the winners.

After the men's college game got a national tournament, more than 40 years passed before the women's college game finally got one, too.

GIRLS JUMP UP

Zero. In 1940, that summed up the NCAA's interest in women's sports. They thought women's basketball was no big deal. After all, it didn't have a big number of players or big stars. But that changed as the women's game grew. From 1970 to 1980, the number of girls who played high school sports in the U.S. climbed from 300,000 to more than 2 million. Basketball topped the list as the most popular game. As the girls went to college, women's college basketball grew, too. Many could handle the ball, shoot, and play just as well as the boys.

Candace Parker, just a freshman at Tennessee, made the first dunk ever in the women's NCAA tournament in 2006. Now she stars for the WNBA's Los Angeles Sparks and for a Euroleague team from Russia.

A CHANCE TO SHINE

By 1981, 880 colleges had women's basketball teams and they were eager to compete. The Association for Intercollegiate Athletics for Women (AIAW) ran a national women's basketball tournament. The final game aired on TV, and the AIAW struck a **lucrative** TV deal for the next few tournaments. Suddenly, women's basketball was a big deal, and the NCAA wanted in. In 1982, the NCAA held a national women's basketball tournament that took off and eventually edged out the AIAW tournament. Today, the NCAA championship game is the highlight of the women's college basketball season.

The Connecticut Huskies have visited with Barack Obama (center) and other presidents after winning a record ten NCAA women's basketball championships.

WADE TROPHY

The Wade Trophy honors the best women's basketball player each year in NCAA Division I, which is the highest level of college sports. The award is named for a hall-of-fame coach, Lily Margaret Wade of Delta State University.

Playing for Connecticut, which is nicknamed UConn, Maya Moore has won the Wade Trophy three times.

17

MARCH MADNESS

Rip-roaring action, stiff competition, and underdogs who snatch championship rings from top dogs. The NCAA college basketball tournament in March has all this and more. No wonder it's called March Madness!

LET THE GAMES BEGIN

Ever heard of the Final Four? Catch March Madness and you will. Every year, 68 teams compete in the men's tournament and 64 teams compete in the women's tournament. Almost half are champions in their conferences. The other half are wild-card teams picked by NCAA members on TV on Selection Sunday before the tournament. The teams are placed in four groups based on their location—East, South, Midwest, and West, then the fun begins. Fans all over the world try to predict the outcome of each game and which teams will make it to the Final Four.

Star centers Frank Kaminsky of the Wisconsin Badgers (left) and Karl-Anthony Towns (12) of the Kentucky Wildcats faced each other in the 2015 Final Four. Towns made this shot, but Wisconsin won the game 71–64.

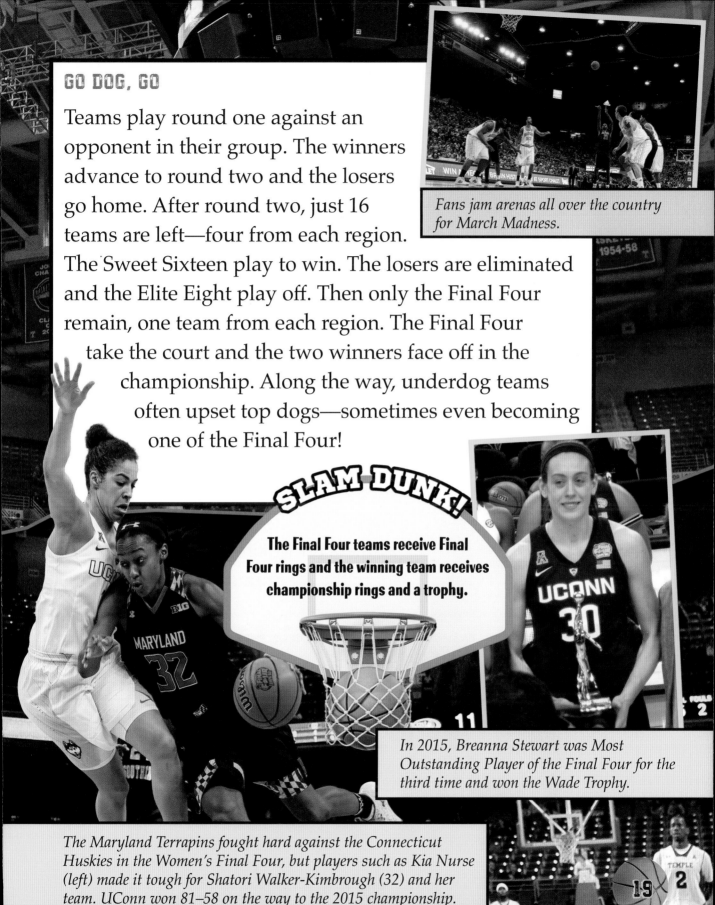

GO DOG, GO

Teams play round one against an opponent in their group. The winners advance to round two and the losers go home. After round two, just 16 teams are left—four from each region. The Sweet Sixteen play to win. The losers are eliminated and the Elite Eight play off. Then only the Final Four remain, one team from each region. The Final Four take the court and the two winners face off in the championship. Along the way, underdog teams often upset top dogs—sometimes even becoming one of the Final Four!

Fans jam arenas all over the country for March Madness.

SLAM DUNK!

The Final Four teams receive Final Four rings and the winning team receives championship rings and a trophy.

In 2015, Breanna Stewart was Most Outstanding Player of the Final Four for the third time and won the Wade Trophy.

The Maryland Terrapins fought hard against the Connecticut Huskies in the Women's Final Four, but players such as Kia Nurse (left) made it tough for Shatori Walker-Kimbrough (32) and her team. UConn won 81–58 on the way to the 2015 championship.

B-BALL'S WORLD CUP

Every four years, basketball rocks and rolls on the international court. Check out how men's and women's national basketball teams vie for the World Cup.

MEN'S WORLD CUP

In 1948, the Olympics' basketball competition was so successful that FIBA decided to hold another world tournament in between the Olympic Games. The men's World Cup was born, and countries rushed to compete. Argentina won the first World Cup. Since then, the United States, **Soviet Union**, Brazil, and Yugoslavia have all won more than once. The tournament is also a slam-dunk hit with fans. In 2010, a record-breaking 800 million people in 171 countries watched the action on TV.

Point guard Kyrie Irving was the floor leader of Team USA and won MVP at the 2014 World Cup.

Team USA celebrated winning the 2014 Men's World Cup in Spain, after big victories in each game.

WOMEN'S WORLD CUP

Just three years after the first men's World Cup, the World Cup of basketball for women bounced onto the scene. Today, national teams from 16 countries battle to win the Cup. But as of 2015, only four have succeeded. They are the powerhouses of women's basketball—the United States, Soviet Union, Brazil, and Australia. In 2014, the United States secured the Cup over Spain in a close game—77 to 64.

THE NAISMITH TROPHY

The FIBA World Cup trophy says "Naismith" like no other. On its base, the flower-shaped trophy made of silver and gold has the name of basketball's inventor engraved in Latin, Arabic, Chinese, and Egyptian **hieroglyphics.**

The women's Team USA also took home the trophy for the 2014 Women's World Cup held in Turkey.

MEN'S OLYMPIC HOOPS

Once basketball became an Olympic sport, nations jumped at the chance to compete. But no country can compete with the United States.

CRUSHING THE COMPETITION

In 1936, the United States took the first Olympic gold medal in men's basketball, beating Canada 19 to 8. The United States went on to win the next six Olympic gold medals too, crushing all teams by winning 54 games straight. But in 1972, the Soviet Union seized the gold medal out of their hands in a **controversial** call. When the final buzzer sounded in the final game between the United States and the Soviet Union, the United States thought they had won, 50 to 49. But officials ruled that the game wasn't over, because the Soviet coach had called a time-out before the ball had been put in play. The Soviets then scored and won.

Team USA sat stunned as the Soviets (left) celebrated in 1972. To this day, people argue about the referees' call.

*Doug Collins, who later became an NBA player, coach, and broadcaster, shot two **free throws** that he thought won the gold for Team USA in 1972.*

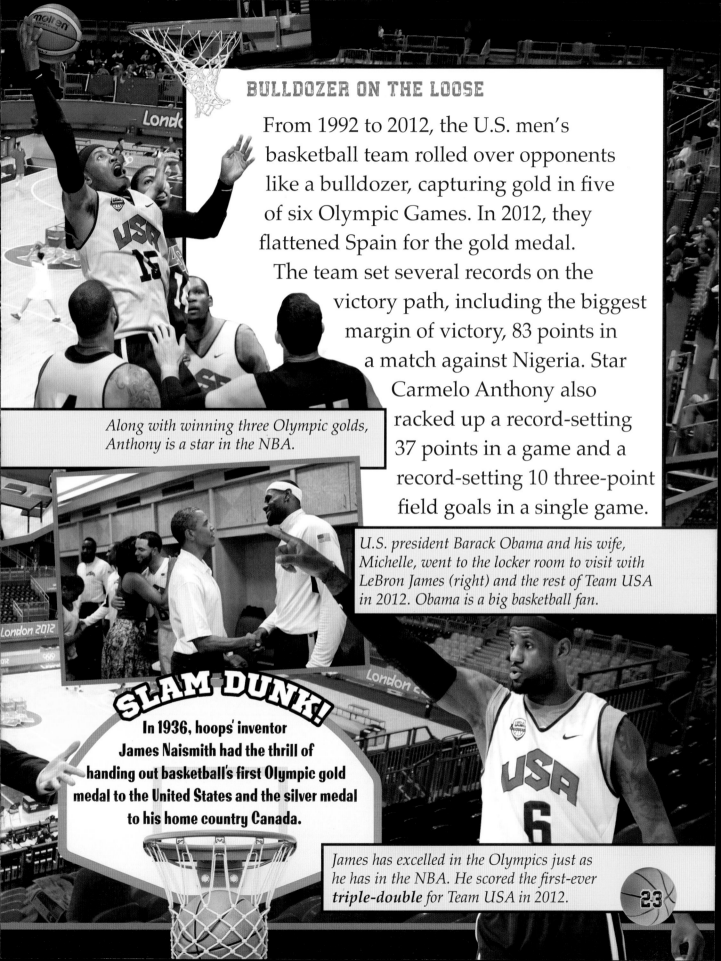

BULLDOZER ON THE LOOSE

From 1992 to 2012, the U.S. men's basketball team rolled over opponents like a bulldozer, capturing gold in five of six Olympic Games. In 2012, they flattened Spain for the gold medal.

The team set several records on the victory path, including the biggest margin of victory, 83 points in a match against Nigeria. Star Carmelo Anthony also racked up a record-setting 37 points in a game and a record-setting 10 three-point field goals in a single game.

Along with winning three Olympic golds, Anthony is a star in the NBA.

U.S. president Barack Obama and his wife, Michelle, went to the locker room to visit with LeBron James (right) and the rest of Team USA in 2012. Obama is a big basketball fan.

SLAM DUNK!

In 1936, hoops' inventor James Naismith had the thrill of handing out basketball's first Olympic gold medal to the United States and the silver medal to his home country Canada.

*James has excelled in the Olympics just as he has in the NBA. He scored the first-ever **triple-double** for Team USA in 2012.*

23

WOMEN'S OLYMPIC HOOPS

In 1976, women's basketball made its debut at the Olympic Games. The competition could not have been fiercer.

GOING FOR THE FIRST OLYMPIC GOLD

The Soviet women's team was a winning machine that hadn't lost a game at a major international competition in 18 years. Team USA were on a roll, too, having just won all their games in the Olympic qualifying rounds. Japan, Czechoslovakia, and Bulgaria were also top contenders. Japan had beaten the United States 84 to 71, but they came back from the loss, defeating Bulgaria and Canada. Then the Soviet Union clobbered them 122 to 77. The Soviets won all their games, taking the gold medal easily. Team USA took silver, and Czechoslovakia bronze.

It's a long road to Olympic gold. First, teams must get through the opening round of group play. The four teams with the best record in each group move on. All the next rounds are winner-take-all. Like the NCAA tournament, there is a round of eight, then a round of four, and finally the championship game for gold. The silver goes to the losing team in that game. The other two teams from the final four play for the bronze medal.

Even though they lost to their main rival in 1976 and their country **boycotted** the 1980 Olympics because of a political dispute with the Soviet Union, Team USA remained determined. In 1984, they took the Olympics by storm, winning the gold medal. They won the gold medal again in 1988 and the bronze in 1992. And they didn't stop there. From 1996 to 2012, Team USA owned the Olympic court, capturing five gold medals in a row. Team USA demolished opponents, beating most by nearly 30 points.

Point guard Sue Bird (6) has been a leader on and off the floor for Team USA. She has won three golds along with two NCAA and two WNBA championships.

TEAM USA RULES

The men's Team USA has taken the gold medal in 14 of the 17 Olympics they have entered, while the women's Team USA has won gold in seven out of nine Olympics. American basketball star Teresa Edwards won a record-setting five Olympic basketball medals—four gold and one bronze.

Edwards was selected for induction into the Naismith Memorial Basketball Hall of Fame in 2011.

PARALYMPIC BASKETBALL

No contest gets rolling quite like Paralympic basketball. Check out how hoopsters all over the world compete on two wheels.

WHEELING AROUND

Around the world, more than 100,000 girls, boys, men, and women play hoops on wheels. Whether they play just for fun or to win for their country, wheelchair basketball is serious fun—and serious competition. Top players go wheel to wheel in international contests, such as the Paralympic Games and the Wheelchair Basketball World Championships held every two years after the Paralympics.

Team Canada (above) celebrated after winning the 2014 Women's World Basketball Championship in front of a home crowd in Toronto (left). Teams from 12 nations competed.

SHOOTING FOR GOLD

The Summer Paralympic Games is the top competition in wheelchair basketball. The Paralympics include tournaments for both men and women, using nearly the same rules as regular basketball. Huge crowds come out to cheer on their favorite teams, and the competition is extreme. The United States, Canada, Australia, Great Britain, Germany, Netherlands, and Japan all have teams that could roll away with a medal. In 2012, the Canadian men won gold over the Australian men, and the German women won gold over the Australian women.

Special wheelchairs have been developed for basketball. They have lowered seats and angled wheels so they will be less likely to tip over during the fast-paced games.

Teams play wheelchair basketball on a standard court and many of the rules are the same. The rules are set by the International Wheelchair Basketball Federation.

SLAM DUNK!

In 1944, Sir Ludwig Guttmann invented an early form of wheelchair basketball to help World War II veterans recover from injuries by rebuilding strength and confidence.

27

BASKETBALL AROUND THE WORLD

Today, the NBA Finals are broadcast in 215 countries in 47 different languages. Additionally, basketball games, leagues, and tournaments are popular on every continent. Check out some highlights of hoops around the globe.

HOOPS IN EUROPE

Every two years, men's and women's national basketball teams from all over Europe and Israel compete at the FIBA EuroBasket. Not only do teams play to win, but they also aim to earn a spot in the Olympics and the FIBA World Cup. In 2012, the European Olympic Committee created the European Games for athletes from all over Europe to compete in a variety of sports every four years.

San Antonio Spurs star Tony Parker also plays in international competitions for France—the country where he grew up. He was MVP of the 2013 Eurobasket, in which France won the gold.

HOOPS IN ASIA AND BEYOND

Basketball 3x3 bounced into the limelight at the Singapore 2010 Youth Olympic Games. It became the hottest sport at the Games and was picked up by players all over the world. Also known as streetball, basketball 3x3 is now the world's largest urban, or city, team sport. In this kind of basketball, two teams of three shoot at the same hoop. Regular basketball games, leagues, and tournaments also pop up in Asia, Africa, and South America. In Asia, for example, China and Japan have pro basketball leagues for men and women. In fact, star players from the Chinese Basketball Association (CBA) have played in the NBA and star NBA players have played for the CBA.

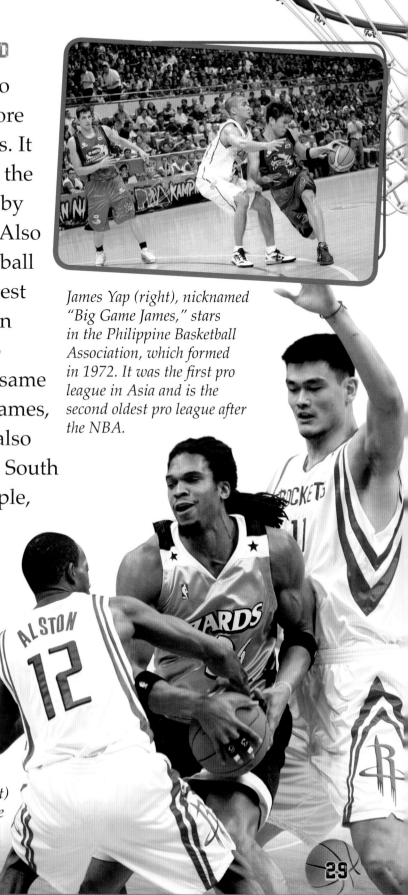

James Yap (right), nicknamed "Big Game James," stars in the Philippine Basketball Association, which formed in 1972. It was the first pro league in Asia and is the second oldest pro league after the NBA.

In 2002, China allowed Yao Ming (right) to jump from the Shanghai Sharks to the Houston Rockets. The 7-foot-6-inch (2.3 m) center became an NBA all-star.

BASKETBALL FANS AND FUTURE STARS

Want to watch some basketball? Just listen for the sound of the bouncing ball, search the Internet for your favorite team to watch their games live online, or go to a game with your friends and family.

GET IN THE GAME

Want to play basketball? Whether you want to be a future b-ball superstar or just have fun, there are lots of ways to get in the game. All you need is a ball, a hoop, and some sneakers. You can shoot hoops indoors or outdoors, on your own, with a friend, or with a couple of friends. You can also join an organized team at the Y or in a local league.

All big stars started playing basketball as kids. Who knows, if you have the love for the game and practice hard, one day you might be "Like Mike."

LEARNING MORE

Check out these books and websites to find out more about the basketball.

BOOKS

The NBA Finals by Drew Silverman, SportsZone, 2013

Great Moments in Olympic Basketball by Doug Williams, SportsZone, 2014

The Final Four: All about College Basketball's Biggest Event by Mary E. Schulte, Capstone Press, 2013

WEBSITES

NBA Hoop Troop

www.nbahooptroop.com

Visit this site to play basketball games, get the most recent scores and stats, and watch videos of players in action.

The International Basketball Federation

www.fiba.com

Photos, videos and information about the FIBA Basketball World Cup. Learn more about international basketball here.

GLOSSARY

Note: Some boldfaced words are defined where they appear in the book.

bank shot A shot that bounces off the backboard and into the basket

boycotted Refused to participate as a way of protesting

caliber Level of excellence or skill

clamoring Making loud and constant noise, often to demand something

controversial Causing public disagreement

folded (sports) Stopped operating due to financial trouble or lack of support

free throw A penalty shot from behind a special line that is worth one point

hieroglyphics A system of writing that uses picture-like symbols

jump shot A shot that is made while jumping

lucrative Profitable, producing wealth

NBA commissioner The person who directs the National Basketball Association

ploy A move designed to fool or trick an opponent

Soviet Union A country in eastern Europe and Asia from 1922 to 1991 that included Russia and was a great rival of the U.S.A.

stable Steady, not changing

standard Authorized or approved

triple-double When a basketball player reaches 10 or more in three categories, usually assists, rebound, and points, in a single game

unruly Unable to be controlled

vie To try hard to win

YMCA Young Men's Christian Association, an organization that promotes health and welfare

INDEX